Collins

Snowdonia
Park Rangers
Favourite Walks

Pa...
Cened...

D1639210

Published by Collins
An imprint of HarperCollins*Publishers*
Westerhill Road, Bishopbriggs, Glasgow G64 2QT
collins.reference@harpercollins.co.uk
www.harpercollins.co.uk

HarperCollins*Publishers*
1st Floor, Watermarque Building, Ringsend Road, Dublin 4, Ireland

Printed in China by RR Donnelley APS Co Ltd

ISBN   978-0-00-843913-2   10 9 8 7 6 5 4 3 2 1

MIX
Paper from
responsible sources
FSC™ C007454

Contents

Conwy Bay
Conwy
Beaumaris
Llanfairfechan
Llansanffra
Glan Conw
A55
Bangor
Bethesda
A5
Caernarfon
Llanrws
Capel
Curig
9
6
Llanberis
Snowdon
Llanwnda
16
1085
10
Betw
y-Coe
Penygroes
8
Blaenau
Ffestiniog
7
Llanaelhaearn
Beddgelert
11
Lleyn
Peninsula
Ffestiniog
Tremadog
19
Criccieth
Porthmadog
Trawsfynyd
Llyn
Trawsfynydd
A470
Pwllheli
Tremadog
Bay
2,3
4
Harlech
15
5
14,1
17
12
1
13
Craig y Ddinas
Barmouth
Llanelltyd
20
Dolgella
Barmouth
Bay
A487
Corr
Tywyn
Machynlleth
A48
Aberdovey
Eglwys
Fach

WALK LOCATIONS

▼ Recommended starting point for each route – refer to individual walk instructions for more details.

A4212

A494 Bala
Bala Lake

Llanuwchllyn

470

Mallwyd A458
Llangadfan

Cader Idris and Tyrrau Mawr are two of the most popular walking peaks in the National Park.

Introduction

The Snowdonia National Park is a special part of the country where people come to relax and enjoy a wide range of leisure activities in spectacular surroundings.

Snowdonia's landscape is unique. The nine mountain ranges cover approximately 52 per cent of the Park and include many peaks that are over 3,000 feet (915 m) high. Apart from the beauty and charm of its high mountains, Snowdonia is a delightfully varied landscape of steep river gorges, waterfalls and green valleys. Oak, ash, rowan and hazel woodlands are found scattered throughout the Park whilst the beautiful Dyfi, Mawddach and Dwyryd estuaries and 23 miles of coastline and sandy beaches contribute to the overall diversity of the landscape.

Snowdonia has many attractions on offer to the visitor from underground audiovisual tours to farm tours, narrow gauge railway trips through breathtaking countryside and for the more adventurous, white water rafting. Whether your stay is for one day or a fortnight, there is always something to see or do.

Snowdonia was designated a National Park in 1951 to safeguard its special qualities. These include breathtaking scenery, deep valleys, lakes, rivers, waterfalls, rugged mountains and fine beaches – Snowdonia has it all. It is also home to over 25,000 people, many of whom work in the National Park where the Welsh language continues to be the predominant language. Each year around 6 million people visit Snowdonia to enjoy these special qualities, and in doing so, contribute greatly to the local economy.

Getting around

If you are looking for a more sustainable and relaxed travel experience than the car then why not take advantage of the local public transport system, cycle routes and walking paths.

There are some great benefits to using a more sustainable form of transport such as local transport for example; reducing carbon footprint and therefore reducing our effect on global warming and climate change. It can also be a chance to enhance the experience of your visit by enabling you to relax and enjoy the views without the added stress of traffic and parking. It can also be a great way to become more immersed within the local community and environment.

Using the train is a great way to get to Snowdonia National Park. Train links exist to locations nearby and within Eryri; Bangor, Betws-Y-Coed, Llanrwst, Conwy, and Llandudno junction, Porthmadog and Blaenau Ffestiniog. You can also make use of the Ffestiniog and Welsh Highlands Railways for a more unique travel experience through parts of Eryri.

Once you are in the National Park you can make use of the local bus services to take you to your desired location. Local bus services include Traws Cymru-Lloyds Coaches, Llew Jones, Arriva Bus Wales, Gwynfor Coaches.

In the heart of the National Park, the Snowdon Sherpa shuttles operate around the base of Yr Wyddfa (Snowdon) connecting all six main footpaths and surrounding villages. If you have travelled to Eryri by car, then why not park up and use the bus for the remaining duration of your trip to travel around Eryri.

Stopped for a rest by Llynnau Cregennen beneath Cader Idris.

Cycling is another great way to travel around Eryri, with many wonderful cycle routes to make the most of whilst visiting the area. There are also many local bike hire facilities, so don't worry if you don't have access to a bike!

If however you do need to visit the National Park by car, please try to car share with other people. If you all arrive and travel around the National Park in a single car instead of separate vehicles, it will save you on fuel and parking costs as well as reducing your carbon footprint.

For more information on travel to and around Snowdonia National Park, please visit one of the many following helpful websites:

http://www.traveline.cymru/#
https://snowdon.live/
Twitter: @visitsnowdonia
Facebook: /eryrisnowdonia
https://www.snowdonia.gov.wales/

Protecting the countryside

Snowdonia National Park Authority wants everyone to enjoy their visit and to help keep the area a special place. You can do this by following the Countryside Code.

There are five sections of the code dedicated to helping members of the public respect, protect and enjoy the countryside. These are:

- Be safe, plan ahead and follow any signs.

- Leave gates and property as you find them.

- Protect plants and animals and take your litter home.

- Keep dogs under close control, especially near farm animals and during the nesting season.

- Consider other people.

The National Park runs a 'Take The Lead' campaign, which encourages responsible dog walking and dogs to be kept on leads around livestock. Walkers should take extra care by sticking to paths during the bird nesting season between 1 March and 15 September.

Call the Snowdonia National Park Headquarters on 01766 770274 or visit our website at **parc@eryri-npa.gov.uk** for more information.

Views of Pen yr Ole Wen from Llyn Idwal.

Walking tips & guidance

Safety

As with all outdoor activities, walking is safe provided a few simple commonsense rules are followed:

- Make sure you are fit enough to complete the walk.

- Always try to let others know where you intend to go.

- Wear sensible clothes and suitable footwear.

- Take a map or guide.

- Always allow plenty of time for the walk and be aware of when it will get dark.

- Walk at a steady pace. A zigzag route is usually a more comfortable way of negotiating a slope. Avoid running directly downhill as it's easier to lose control and may also cause erosion to the hillside.

- When walking on country roads, walk on the right-hand side facing the oncoming traffic, unless approaching a blind bend, when you should cross over to the left so as to be seen from both directions.

- Try not to dislodge stones on high edges or slopes.

- If the weather changes unexpectedly and visibility becomes poor, don't panic, but try to remember the last certain feature you passed and work out your route from that point on the map. Be sure of your route before continuing.

Unfortunately, accidents can happen even on easy walks. If you're with someone who has an accident or can't continue, you should:

- Make sure the injured person is sheltered from further injury, although you should never move anyone with a head, neck or back injury.

- If you have a phone with a signal, call for help.

- If you can't get a signal and have to leave the injured person to go for help, try to leave a note saying what has happened and what first aid you have tried. Make sure you know the exact location so you can give accurate directions to the emergency services. When you reach a telephone call 999 and ask for the police or mountain rescue.

Equipment
The equipment you will need depends on several factors, such as the type of activity planned, the time of year, and the weather likely to be encountered.

Clothing should be adequate for the day. In summer, remember sun screen, especially for your head and neck. Wear light woollen socks and lightweight boots or strong shoes. Even on hot days take an extra layer and waterproofs in your rucksack, just in case.

Winter wear is a much more serious affair. Remember that once the body starts to lose heat, it becomes much less efficient. Jeans are particularly unsuitable for winter walking.

When considering waterproof clothing, it pays to buy the best you can afford. Make sure that the jacket is loose-fitting, windproof and has a generous hood. Waterproof overtrousers will not only offer protection against the rain, but they are also windproof. Clothing described as 'showerproof' will not keep you dry in heavy rain, and those made from rubberized or plastic materials can be heavy to carry and will trap moisture on the inside. Your rucksack should have wide, padded carrying straps for comfort.

It is important to wear boots that fit well or shoes with a good moulded sole – blisters can ruin any walk! Woollen socks are much more comfortable than any other fibre. Your clothes should be comfortable and not likely to catch on twigs and bushes.

It is important to carry a compass and a map or guide. A small first aid kit is also useful for treating cuts and other small injuries.

Finally, take a bottle of water and enough food to keep you going.

Public rights of way

Right of way means that anyone may walk freely on a defined footpath or ride a horse or bicycle along a public bridleway. In 1949, the National Parks and Access to the Countryside Act tidied up the law covering rights of way. Following public consultation, maps were drawn up by the Countryside Authorities of England and Wales to show all rights of way. Copies of these maps are available for public inspection and are invaluable when trying to resolve doubts over little-used footpaths. Once on the map, the right of way is irrefutable.

Any obstructions to a right of way should be reported to the local Highways Authority.

In England and Wales rights of way fall into three main categories:

- Public footpaths – for walkers only.

- Bridleways – for passage on foot, horseback or bicycle.

- Byways – for all the above and for motorized vehicles.

Free access to footpaths and bridleways does mean that certain guidelines should be followed as a courtesy to those who live and work in the area. For example, you should only sit down to picnic where it does not interfere with other walkers or the landowner. All gates must be kept closed to prevent stock from straying and dogs must be kept under close control – usually this is interpreted as meaning that they should be kept on a lead. Motorised vehicles must not be driven along a public footpath or bridleway without the landowner's consent.

A farmer may put a docile mature beef bull with a herd of cows or heifers, in a field crossed by a public footpath. Beef bulls such as Herefords (usually brown/red in colour) are unlikely to be upset by passers-by but dairy bulls, like the black-and-white Friesian, can be dangerous by nature. It is, therefore, illegal for a farmer to let a dairy bull roam loose in a field open to public access.

The Countryside and Rights of Way Act 2000 (the 'right to roam') allows access on foot to areas of legally defined 'open country' – mountain, moor, downland, heath and registered common land. It does not allow freedom to walk everywhere. It also increases protection for Sites of Special Scientific Interest, improves wildlife enforcement legislation and allows for better management of Areas of Outstanding Natural Beauty.

How to use this book

Each of the walks in this guide are set out in a similar way. They are all introduced with a simple locator map followed by a brief description of the area, its geography and history, and some notes on things you will encounter on your walk.

Near the start of each section there is a panel of information outlining the distance of the walk, the time it is expected to take and briefly describing the path conditions or the terrain you will encounter. A suggested starting point, along with grid reference is shown, as is the nearest postcode – although in rural locations postcodes can cover a large area and are therefore only a rough guide for sat nav users. It is always sensible to take a reference map with you, and the relevant OS Explorer map is also listed.

The major part of each section is taken up with a plan for each walk and detailed point by point, description of our recommended route, along with navigational tips and points of interest.

Here is a description of the main symbols on the route maps:

	Motorway	🚇	Railway station	30m	Contour height (m)
	Trunk/primary road	🚌	Bus station/stop		Walk route
	Secondary road	🚗	Car park		Optional route
	Tertiary road	🏰	Castle	❶	Route instruction
	Residential/ unclassified road	†	Church		Open land
	Service road	⛯	Lighthouse		Park/sports ground
	Track	★	Interesting feature		Urban area
	Pedestrian/ bridleway/cycleway	*i*	Tourist information		Woodland
	Footway/path	☕	Café		Nature reserve
	Railway	🍺	Pub		Wetland
	River/coast	🚻	Toilets		Lake

WALK 1
Abergwynant Woods

The native woodland environment combined with far-reaching views of the Mawddach Estuary makes this walk a perfect way to enjoy a leisurely morning or afternoon.

Abergwynant Woods is a native woodland on the southern side of the Mawddach estuary, and is owned and managed by the National Park Authority. The woodland is made up of a diverse range of tree species including oak, birch, ash, rowan, sycamore and holly, and in late spring the woodland floor is carpeted with bluebells. The area attracts many bird species, including black cap, wood warbler, long tailed tit, tawny owl, and in the springtime, pied fly catchers.

The circular walk also follows part of the beautiful Mawddach Trail, which runs along the former track bed of the Ruabon–Barmouth Great Western Railway line. The railway opened in 1865 and closed a hundred years later under the Beeching Axe. Popular with visitors, the railway was also used briefly to carry slate from the nearby quarry at Arthog. Another clue to the area's industrial past can be seen in the remains of an old lime kiln on the bank of the Afon Gwynant river.

1 From the car park at Penmaenpool, walk past the toilet block and former railway signal box, and cross the road near the timber toll bridge. Continue straight ahead along the tarmac road past the George III hotel, which will eventually become a gravel track.

2 Continue straight ahead for around a mile (1.6 km), until you reach a picnic table and a gate on the left-hand side of the track.

Go through the gate and climb the zigzag path up through Abergwynant Woods.

3 The path climbs gradually to the top of the hill. When you reach a fork in the path, bear right and follow a short section of path that leads to a picnic area with a spectacular view of the Mawddach estuary and Barmouth beyond.

4 Retrace your steps from the picnic area and bear right at the fork in the path. When you reach another fork, bear left and follow the path up through the woodland.

5 Keep left as you join another path. Follow the path down through the woods with care, especially when wet. Below on the left you will see Abergwynant Hall.

6 As the path levels out follow the track which runs alongside Afon Gwynant river. Keep an eye out for the old lime kiln on the left on the riverbank.

7 Once past the lime kiln, bear right at the fork and follow the narrow path uphill.

8 When the path re-joins the track, bear right and follow the track past an old sawmill.

9 Continue straight ahead and follow the path down to the left before the gate in front of you.

10 When you reach a fork in the path bear left, and then bear right at the next fork to retrace your steps back down to the Mawddach Trail.

11 Once back on the Mawddach Trail, bear right and continue straight ahead until you arrive back at the car park.

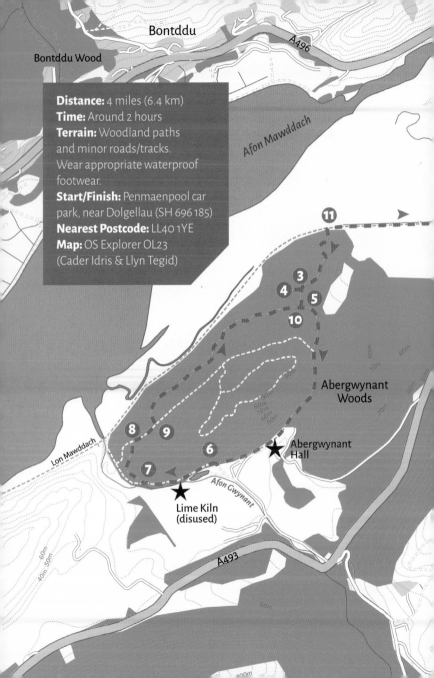

Bontddu

Bontddu Wood

A496

Afon Mawddach

Distance: 4 miles (6.4 km)
Time: Around 2 hours
Terrain: Woodland paths
and minor roads/tracks.
Wear appropriate waterproof
footwear.
Start/Finish: Penmaenpool car
park, near Dolgellau (SH 696 185)
Nearest Postcode: LL40 1YE
Map: OS Explorer OL23
(Cader Idris & Llyn Tegid)

11

3

4

5

10

Abergwynant
Woods

80m

70m

80m

70m

60m

50m

80m
70m
60m
50m

8

9

6

★ Abergwynant
Hall

Lon Mawddach

7

Afon Gwynant

★ Lime Kiln
(disused)

A493

60m
40m 50m

60m

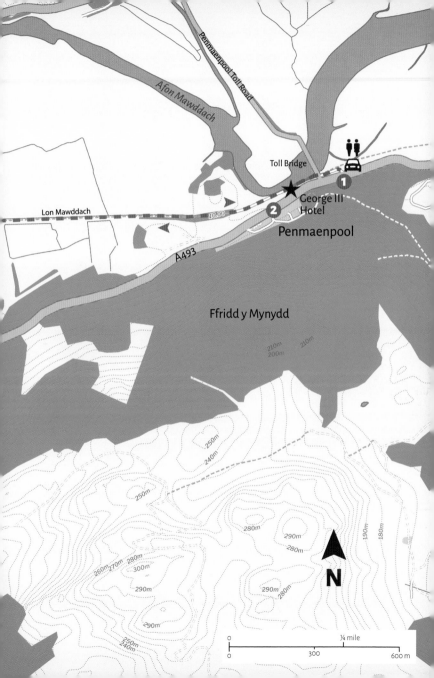

The woodland paths are well marked with information on the flora and fauna that you might see on your walk.

Coed Abergwynant

WALK 2
Bwlch Drws Ardudwy

The Rhinogydd and surrounding area is considered one of the last remaining areas of true wilderness in Wales.

This is the perfect walk if you want to escape the crowds and spend an hour or two enjoying complete peace and tranquility. Take some binoculars to make the most of the stunning panoramic views and the opportunities for birdwatching.

The longer of two walks in the area (see Coed Graigddu walk), this circular route will take you to Bwlch Drws Ardudwy (translated as 'the doorway to Ardudwy'), which is the pass between the mountains of Rhinog Fawr and Rhinog Fach. This walk will allow you to experience the rugged beauty of Rhinogydd National Nature Reserve and Graigddu woodland.

As well as being an ideal habitat for a wealth of biodiversity, for over fifty years this area has been home to a herd of wild ponies! They were originally bred as pit ponies, but with advances in technology the demand for these ponies decreased, and with time they became feral. They are quite shy creatures, who are not very fond of being touched. Be vigilant and keep your distance if there are stallions about as they can run wild and fight each other fiercely over a foal!

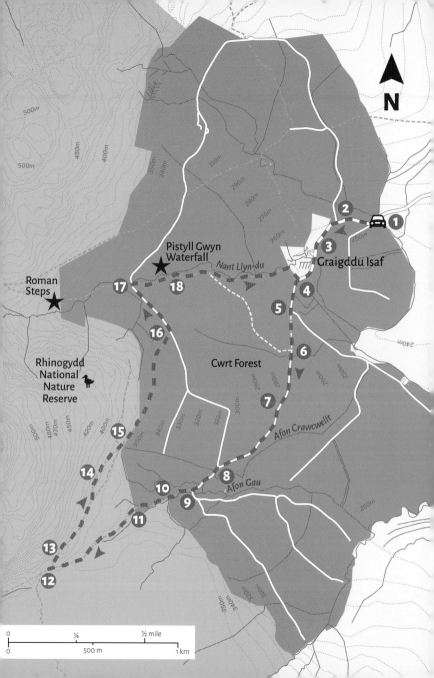

Roman
Steps

Rhinogydd
National
Nature
Reserve

Pistyll Gwyn
Waterfall

Nant Llyn-du

Graigddu Isaf

Cwrt Forest

Afon Crawcwellt

Afon Gau

N

1
2
3
4
5
6
7
8
9
10
11
12
13
14
15
16
17
18

0   ¼   ½ mile
0   500 m   1 km

Distance: 4 miles (6.4 km)
Time: Around 2 hours
Terrain: Mountain heathland and some rough, wet terrain. Wear appropriate footwear.
Start/Finish: Coed Graigddu car park (SH 684 302)
Nearest Postcode: LL40 2LB
Map: OS Eplorer OL18 (Harlech, Porthmadog & Bala)

1 From the Coed Graigddu car park, follow the gravel track on the right, signposted Bwlch Drws Ardudwy.

2 After about 200 m, bear left at the first junction along the gravel track.

3 Mind the animals as you walk past Graigddu Isaf on your right. Keep left of the farmhouse and cross the bridge straight ahead.

4 Soon you will see a signpost to your right for Bwlch Tyddiad (Roman Steps). Do not take this path, but instead keep on following the Bwlch Drws Ardudwy path.

5 After a further 200 m, follow the path to the right (go around the locked gate).

6 In a while you will see a turning on your right – continue straight ahead here, without taking the turning.

7 Continue along the track for just over half a mile (around 1 km).

8 At the next junction follow the track to the left, following the sign for Bwlch Drws Ardudwy.

9 After another 200 m bear right, following the sign for Bwlch Drws Ardudwy.

10 Continue up the path for nearly a quarter of a mile (around 350 m).

11 Go through the gate and enter the Rhinogydd National Nature Reserve (NNR). The terrain will now be more rugged, and can become wet underfoot.

12 After a third of a mile (about 600 m), take a sharp right around 50 m or so before a stone wall.

13 Continue up towards a saddle in the ridge.

14 Once you've reached the top of the hill, follow the path down and after almost half a mile (around 750 m) climb over the fence using the appropriate steps.

15 Follow the path along the edge of the tree plantation until you reach a stile. Climb over the stile and follow the path to your left.

16 Continue along the path through the plantation for nearly a third of a mile (500 m) until you reach a junction. Turn left and continue along a wider track.

17 Soon you will reach a junction. Bear right and take the path that follows the river downhill.

18 After almost a third of a mile (500 m) you will see the Pistyll Gwyn waterfall on your left. After the same distance again you will reach a T-junction – bear left and re-trace your steps back to the car park.

WALK 3
Coed Graigddu

This walk along forest tracks makes it relatively easy on the legs and feet, but the sense of being surrounded by tranquillity and wilderness prevails.

The shorter of two walks in the area (see Bwlch Drws Ardudwy Walk for the longer version), this circular walk follows quiet forest tracks. You will also pass the small but picturesque Pistyll Gwyn waterfall and see some spectacular views of the Rhinogydd mountain range to the west, and Cader Idris to the south.

The pass seen between Rhinog Fawr and Rhinog Fach is called Bwlch Drws Ardudwy ('the doorway to Ardudwy'), and to the right is Bwlch Tyddiad, also known as the Roman Steps. Despite the name, this flagstone path only dates back as far as the medieval period, and was constructed to facilitate access for pack animals from the hinterland onto the coastal plains of Ardudwy.

This wild habitat is a haven for wildlife, so a pair of binoculars is a must! The terrain can be a bit steep in places, so make sure you wear appropriate footwear.

Distance: 3 miles (4.8 km) circular walk

Time: Around 1 hour

Terrain: Gravel tracks and some rough, wet terrain.

Start/Finish: Coed Graigddu car park (SH 684 302)

Nearest Postcode: LL40 2LB

Map: OS Explorer OL18 (Harlech, Porthmadog & Bala)

1 From the Coed Graigddu car park, follow the gravel track on the right, signposted Bwlch Drws Ardudwy.

2 After 200 m, bear left at the first junction along the gravel track.

3 Mind the animals as you walk past Graigddu Isaf on your right. Keep left of the farmhouse and cross the bridge straight ahead.

4 Soon you will see a signpost to your right for Bwlch Tyddiad (Roman Steps). Do not take this path, but instead keep on following the Bwlch Drws Ardudwy path.

5 After a further 200 m, follow the path to the right (go around the locked gate).

6 In a while you will see a turning on your right – continue straight ahead here, without taking the turning.

7 Continue along the track for just over half a mile (around 1 km).

8 At the next junction take the track to the right – do not follow the Bwlch Drws Ardudwy wooden fingerpost.

9 Continue up the track and after about a third of a mile (600 m) follow the track around to the right.

10 Keep following the path through the tree plantation for a further 300 m.

11 Soon you will reach a junction. Bear right and follow the waymarker for Pistyll Gwyn.

12 After almost a third of a mile (500 m) you will see the Pistyll Gwyn waterfall on your left. After the same distance again you will reach a T-junction – bear left and retrace your steps back to the car park.

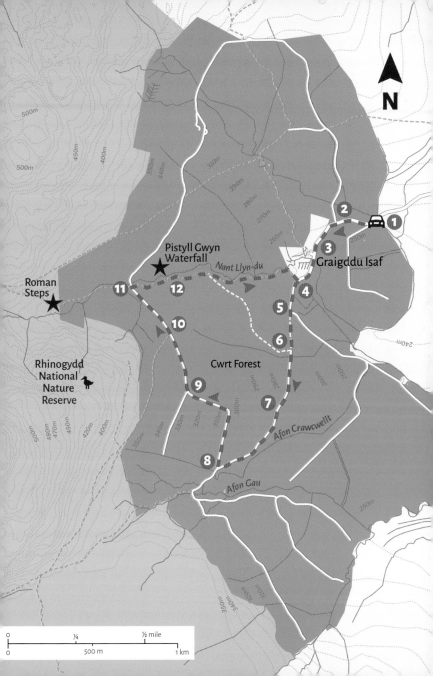

Pistyll Gwyn
Waterfall

Nant Llyn-du

Roman
Steps

Graigddu Isaf

Cwrt Forest

Rhinogydd
National
Nature
Reserve

Afon Crawcwellt

Afon Gau

500m
450m
400m
500m
350m
340m
310m
290m
280m
270m
260m
250m
240m
290m
280m
260m
250m
480m
470m
450m
420m
400m
500m
350m
340m
330m
320m
310m
300m
340m
330m
320m
310m
300m
290m
280m
250m
250m
320m
310m
340m

N

1
2
3
4
5
6
7
8
9
10
11
12

0   ¼   ½ mile
0   500 m   1 km

WALK 4
Craig y Penmaen

A delightful walk steeped in history, offering breathtaking views of the Rhinogydd mountain range and the Cwm Cain valley.

This delightful, leisurely circular route combines spectacular views of the Rhinogydd and Llyn Trawsfynydd with the enclosed atmosphere of the Coed y Brenin forest. The walk starts at Penstryd chapel, and climbs gradually along the western flank of Craig y Penmaen. The route follows part of Sarn Helen, the old Roman road into Coed y Brenin, before crossing Afon Gain river and returning along Cwm Cain to the east of Craig y Penmaen.

For much of the first half of the twentieth century this area was occupied by the British Army and used as a military artillery range and training camp. The bare heathland to the east is still known locally as the Ranges, and some structural remains of this period can be seen dotted around the area to this day.

1 From Penstryd chapel, go through the gate over the road opposite and follow the Sarn Helen track up towards Craig y Penmaen. From here you can enjoy wonderful views of the Arenig to the east, the Aran and Rhobell, and through Cwm Cain towards Coed y Brenin.

2 Go through another gate to Ffridd Tyddyn Du, passing an old military observatory – one of numerous remains of the former military camp. From the top of the hill you can enjoy a spectacular panoramic view of the Rhinogydd mountain range.

Distance: 4½ miles (7.25 km (with optional 1-mile (1.6-km) extension)
Time: Around 2–3 hours (+ around ½ hour for the optional extension)
Terrain: Tarmac road and tracks.
Start/Finish: Penstryd, Bronaber (SH 726 318)
Nearest Postcode: LL41 4UY
Map: OS Explorer OL18 (Harlech, Porthmadog & Bala)

3 Follow the track (Sarn Helen) which runs along the western flank of Craig y Penmaen. After about a mile (1.6 km) you will reach the northern edge of Coed y Brenin, where you can see the path dropping quite steeply. Look out for the milestone in the wall on your left showing the distances to Dolgellau and Trawsfynydd.

4 Turn left off Sarn Helen, which is now part of the forest track, and go through a wooden gate into a wooded area. Follow the path past the ruins of 'Penmaen', then join the forest track above Afon Gain river. Follow the track to the left.

5 Shortly, a public footpath on the right will take you towards Afon Gain. Follow this path through the woods and cross the footbridge over the river. Follow the path and join the forest track. Turn left and keep following the track for some time until you join the tarmac road at the bottom of Moel Gwynfynydd.

6 Follow the tarmac road to the left, up Cwm Cain with Craig y Penmaen on your left. In around a mile (1.6 km) you will cross a beautiful picturesque bridge over Afon Gain. The bridge is known locally as Pont Llyn Du, which means the 'bridge over the black pool'. After crossing the bridge the road will climb steeply towards Penstryd chapel and back to the start.

Optional extension: If you would like to extend the route, you can follow a permissive path over farmland which will take you past Llech Idris, a large upright slab in a field. To follow this route, walk up the road from Pont Llyn Du, and look out for the entrance to Dolgain farm on the left. **7** Opposite the farm entrance there is a permissive path which leads across the field, past Llech Idris and on to the Abergeirw road. Turn left onto the tarmac road and keep bearing left until you eventually come to a shortcut that will take you back to Penstryd chapel. Note that the path through the fields can be quite wet underfoot.

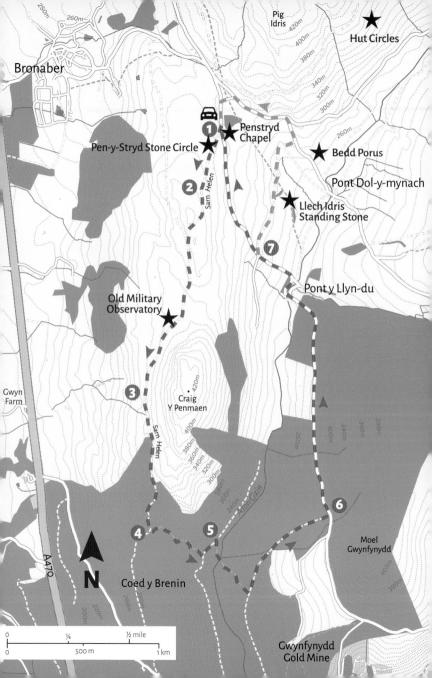

Pig
Idris

★ **Hut Circles**

Bronaber

🚗

① ★ Penstryd
      Chapel

Pen-y-Stryd Stone Circle ★

②   ★ **Bedd Porus**

                                     Pont Dol-y-mynach

                              ★ **Llech Idris
                                   Standing Stone**

                                 ⑦

                                        Pont y Llyn-du

**Old Military
Observatory** ★

Gwyn
Farm

③
                  • Craig
                     Y Penmaen

                                                        ⑥
                                              Moel
                                              Gwynfynydd

④   ⑤

▲
N   Coed y Brenin

A470

Gwynfynydd
Gold Mine

Sarn Helen

Afon Gain

0	¼	½ mile
0	500 m	1 km

A clear day offers stunning views of the Rhinogydd mountain range.

WALK 5
Craig y Ddinas

The Ardudwy area is mottled with archeological remains — from round houses and hillforts, to Neolithic burial chambers.

Standing on an isolated rock 1,150 ft (350 m) above sea level, the site of the Iron Age hillfort at Craig y Ddinas offers a fascinating opportunity to explore the archeological remains as well as taking in the spectacular panoramic views of both sea and mountains.

The site occupies a wide upland valley overlooked by the mountains of Moelfre, Diffwys and Llawlech. The oval-shaped hillfort is well preserved, especially around the external side of the fort where some of the stone ramparts can be seen in their original state. There's an impressive entrance on the eastern side of the hillfort with a trackway defined by stone walls leading down to flatter ground where the remains of round houses from the Iron Age and the Roman periods can be seen. Whether you want to explore the prehistoric remains or enjoy the fine views, you will be greatly rewarded by this walk.

1 Turn right out of the car park at Cors-y-gedol and follow the track straight ahead through two gates. The fields on your right are a multi-period landscape containing the remains of ancient field systems and settlements. There is a Neolithic burial cairn as well as Bronze Age burnt-stone mounds, prehistoric huts, two Romano-British hut groups and numerous medieval and post-medieval building foundations, all illustrating how favourable an environment this has been for our ancestors.

2 Continue along the track , which takes you past the remains of Cors-uchaf on your left. On a sunny day, there are fine views of the mountains and sea.

3 Shortly, you will reach two gates that are side by side. Go through the gate on the right, and the track immediately bears right. When the track winds to the left you will see Craig y Ddinas to the right in the distance and, behind the hillfort, the Llawlech ridge.

4 The track climbs gradually towards the slopes of Moelfre. Go through the gate and after less than a third of a mile (500 m) you will reach another gate that opens on to open access land.

5 Walk along the track for a third of a mile (500 m) then turn right and head southwest towards a stile over a stone wall around 300 m away. This section can be very wet and boggy at times.

6 Go over the stile and continue for another 300 m or so towards Craig y Ddinas hillfort.

7 When you reach the hillfort, take time to explore and enjoy the views. From the entrance on the eastern side, walk down the trackway and explore the remains of the round houses on the flatter land below. To return to the start of the walk, retrace your steps back to the track. Turn left and follow the track back to the car park.

Distance: Linear route, 4 miles (6.4 km) there and back
Time: Around 2–3 hours
Terrain: Mainly tracks which can be boggy in places.
Start/Finish: Car park (fee) near Cors y Gedol Hall, Dyffryn Ardudwy (SH 602 231)
Nearest Postcode: LL44 2RJ
Map: OS Explorer OL18 (Harlech, Porthmadog & Bala)

Tal y Ffynonau

★ Stone Circle

250m

240 m

230m

Cors-uchaf ★ ③

②

210m

200m

Cors-y-gedol Hall

★

① 🚗

➤

Cors-y-gedol

Cors-y-Gedol Ancient Settlement

★ Burial Chamber

Burial Chamber ★

180m

Ffordd Ffridd Isa

170m

160m

150m

Coed Cors-y-gedol

Pont Fadog

0 ¼ mile
0 250 500 m

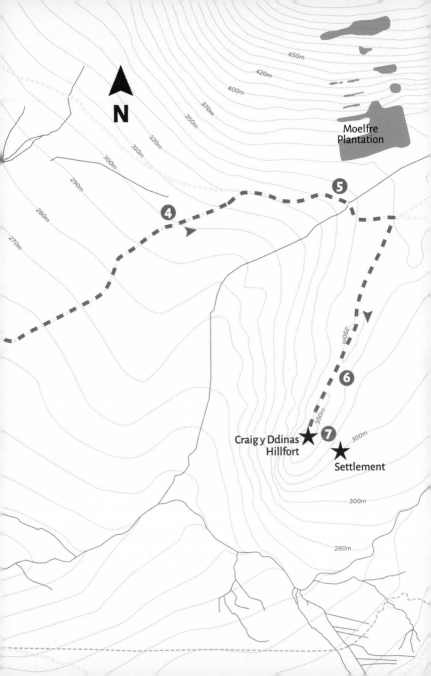

Evidence of human activity spanning thousands of years can be seen on the walk.

WALK 6
Crimpiau

This is a perfect walk for those who want to experience the highlands of Snowdonia and enjoy far-reaching views without venturing up the highest peaks.

From the tranquil summit of Crimpiau near Capel Curig in the north of the Snowdonia National Park you can enjoy magnificent panoramic views of the Snowdon horseshoe and Mymbyr valley, the rugged ridge of Tryfan and the Glyderau overlooking the Ogwen valley. To the northeast, at the foothills of Creigiau Gleision and on the edge of the Carneddau mountain range, lies the beautiful reservoir of Llyn Crafnant.

Binoculars are a must if you want to make the most of the fascinating variety of landscapes and habitats you will pass along this circular walk, from beautiful native woodland to heathland and open moorland, which is an ideal habitat for all kinds of plant and animal species.

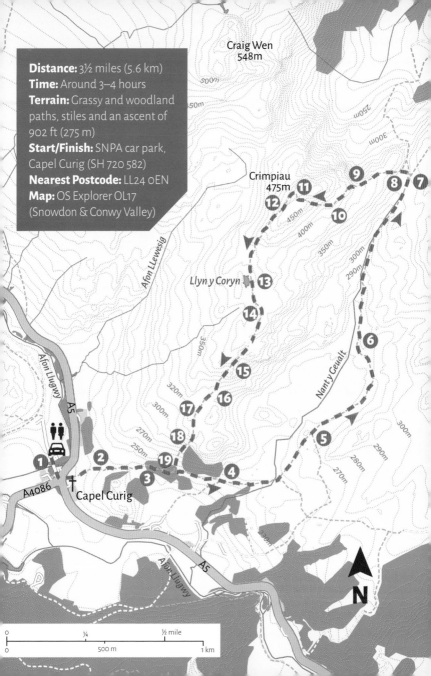

Distance: 3½ miles (5.6 km)
Time: Around 3–4 hours
Terrain: Grassy and woodland paths, stiles and an ascent of 902 ft (275 m)
Start/Finish: SNPA car park, Capel Curig (SH 720 582)
Nearest Postcode: LL24 0EN
Map: OS Explorer OL17 (Snowdon & Conwy Valley)

Craig Wen
548m

Crimpiau
475m

Afon Llewesig

Llyn y Coryn

Nant y Ceualt

Afon Llugwy

A5

Capel Curig

A4086

Afon Llugwy

A5

N

0   ¼   ½ mile
0   500 m   1 km

1 From the car park at Capel Curig, make your way back to the main road and walk up the track to the left of St Curig's Church opposite the junction.

2 At the top of the track go through a gap in the wall and bear right to cross a small stone clapper bridge. Follow the stone pitched path across the field.

3 Climb over the stile and follow the path through a beautiful woodland. When the path seems to fork, follow the path down to the right towards a gap in the wall.

4 Continue along the path and out of the woodland, over a stile, and continue until you cross a wooden bridge. Turn left immediately after crossing the bridge.

5 Follow the path over a hillock for about a third of a mile (500 m) and climb over the stile.

6 Continue along the path for another third of a mile (500 m). Cross the small stream and climb over the stile. Follow the path to the right, keeping the crags of Creigiau Geuallt to your left.

7 After a little more than half a mile (1 km), the path reaches a fork. Bear left and pass a large boulder on your right.

8 Keep following the path until you reach a crossroad of narrow paths. Turn left through the rushes.

9 Begin your ascent to the summit of Crimpiau, taking care on the steep and rocky terrain..

10 Once Llyn Crafnant comes into sight, bear right and follow the path up a steep slope.

11 Continue climbing, and then straight ahead over a flat, boggy area. The path to the summit leads up to the right. Take care on this section as it is very loose underfoot. Once you have reached the summit, take time to enjoy the panoramic views.

12 Begin your descent by following the path along the right side of the ridge, southwest of the summit.

13 After a third of a mile (500 m) you will come to a small lake called Llyn y Coryn. Keeping the lake on your right, continue along the path.

14 Once past the lake, aim for a wire fence on the horizon up on the right. Climb over a short rocky section of path, keeping the wire fence on your right.

15 Follow the path down a steep slope. Keeping the wire stock fence on your right, continue on the path, climbing over two stiles.

16 After the second stile, turn right keeping the wire fence on your right.

17 Walk over wet, boggy terrain, keeping the fence on your right, and continue over the stile on the right.

18 Continue down the path to another stile on the left, climb over and make your way down a very steep slope. At the bottom of the slope you will rejoin the path near the starting point of the walk.

19 Turn right and retrace your footsteps back to Capel Curig.

The climb to the summit of Crimpiau is rewarded by the spectacular views across Snowdonia.

WALK 7
Croesor

A delightful walk beginning at the remote upland hamlet of Croesor, offering spectacular and far-reaching views of mountains and sea.

This circular walk begins at the remote upland village of Croesor, nestling on the foothills of Cnicht, nicknamed the Welsh Matterhorn. The route will take you down through Cwm Croesor valley, past the former Parc Quarry, to the lowlands near the Glaslyn estuary.

Parc Quarry opened in 1870, under the management of engineer Moses Kellow. Both Parc Quarry and Croesor Quarry were jointly operated, producing around 5,000 tonnes of slate each year. Both underground, the quarries were renowned for their use of technical innovations such as electric locomotives and a patented rock drill. In their heyday the quarries employed fifty men, but Parc quarry closed in 1920 and Croesor Quarry in 1930.

You will make your way back up to Croesor along the Afon Croesor river initially, then climb up through a native woodland before emerging on the top of the northern flank of Cwm Croesor, from where the views are spectacular.

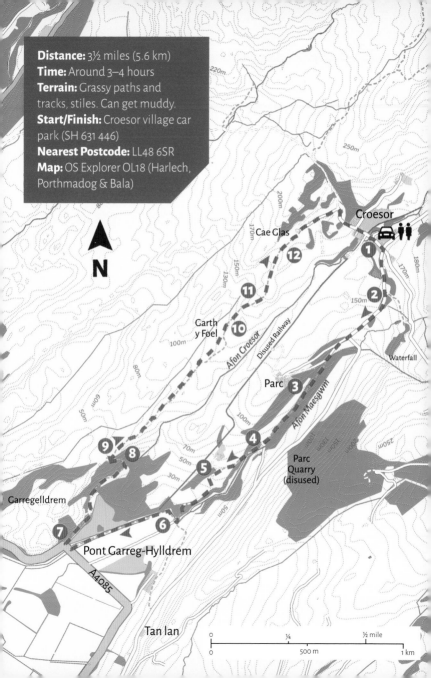

Distance: 3½ miles (5.6 km)
Time: Around 3–4 hours
Terrain: Grassy paths and tracks, stiles. Can get muddy.
Start/Finish: Croesor village car park (SH 631 446)
Nearest Postcode: LL48 6SR
Map: OS Explorer OL18 (Harlech, Porthmadog & Bala)

N

Croesor

Cae Glas

12

1

2

11

Garth y Foel

10

Afon Croesor

Disused Railway

Waterfall

Parc

3

Afon Maesgwm

4

9

8

5

Parc Quarry (disused)

Garregelldrem

7

6

Pont Garreg-Hylldrem

A4085

Tan lan

0   ¼   ½ mile

0   500 m   1 km

1 Turn left at the car park entrance in Croesor and follow the tarmac road towards the crossroad, then taking the road downhill to the right. At the sharp left-hand bend in the road, continue straight ahead along the track, making your way through a gate on your left.

2 Follow the track for around 100 m and then down the footpath to the left. To your left is Afon Maesgwm river. Keep walking downhill, through a gate, keeping the river on your right. Be careful here as this section can become wet and boggy.

3 You'll shortly come out onto a brief clearing. Keep left here. Down on your left you'll see the remnants of the old Parc Quarry.

4 As you pass the quarry you'll reach a house, known locally as Office Ceunant. Walk past the house and make your way through the gate. Follow the footpath as it rises above the river. Take care on this section as it can get quite slippery, and beware of the drop on your left. As you rise above the river, head towards the kissing gate then deviate right and walk through the field, following the waymarker.

5 You'll shortly reach a track – follow it downhill and over a small stone bridge over Afon Maesgwm. Turn right and follow the footpath along the riverbank.

6 Continue along the river until you reach the main road. Turn right, taking extra care as it can be busy with traffic, and walk over the bridge, turning right again onto a track leading to Felin Parc.

7 Walk along the track with Afon Croesor river on your right. On your left you'll see Tan-y-Clogwyn house. Keep walking uphill past Felin Parc on your right-hand side. Follow the waymarker off the track and onto a footpath, past Gelli cottage on the right.

8 Make your way up through the woods until you reach a clearing. Bear right and go through a gap in the wall where you will emerge on to the ridgeline.

9 Follow the footpath along the ridge until you reach a gate in a stone wall ahead of you. Go through the gate and continue towards the fallen tree and through a gap in the wall. Walk on, and follow the footpath to the left, avoiding the gap in the wall on the right as you walk towards Garth y Foel house ahead.

10 Follow the path to the left of Garth y Foel towards the outbuildings, where you will see a wooden gate between them. Go through the gate and make your way uphill, turning right at the top of the hill.

11 Aim for the stile at the far end of the field and climb over, continuing through the tree plantation and through a wooden gate. Keep walking ahead and through a metal gate into the next field.

12 Head towards Cae Glas farmhouse and follow the permissive path through a gate on your right and then another gate on the left past the outbuildings. Go past the front of the property and follow the track to the road. Turn right here and follow the road back to Croesor.

The distinctive summit of Cnicht takes its name from 'Knight', since its shape is said to resemble that of a knight's helmet.

WALK 8

Cwm Bychan and Fisherman's Path

From dramatic landscapes and glorious far-reaching views, to the remains of a former mining industry – this walk has it all!

This circular walk starts in the picturesque village of Beddgelert and follows the Glaslyn river through the dramatic Aberglaslyn pass, before climbing up through Cwm Bychan past the remains of the area's former mining industry. The route then drops down to Llyn Dinas, returning to Beddgelert along the Afon Glaslyn river and past the restored Sygun Copper Mine visitor attraction.

Small-scale mining in the Beddgelert area was begun during the Roman occupation, but the small tunnels into mineral veins were then left relatively untouched until the Industrial Revolution. In Cwm Bychan, you can see the remains of a cable car system used to transport copper ore down from the hills. The ore was then taken by horse and cart to Porthmadog, from where it was shipped to Swansea for refining into copper.

❶ In Beddgelert, walk along the car park approach road and turn left past the Information Centre, heading for the bridge in the village centre. Don't cross the bridge, but follow the narrow road down the riverside to the right.

❷ After passing the public toilets, go through the gate on the right before the footbridge and follow the riverside path. Continue straight ahead until you reach a footbridge and railway.

Distance: 6 miles (9.6 km)
Time: Around 4–6 hours
Terrain: Some steep, rough and wet sections.
Start/Finish: SNPA car park Beddgelert, near the Information Centre (SH 588 481)
Nearest Postcode: LL55 4YJ
Map: OS Explorer OL17 (Snowdon & Conwy Valley)

N

450m
420m
400m
380m
350m
300m
280m
250m
200m

Coed
Pant-agored

Llyn
Dinas

Coed
Maes-llifio

Dinas
Emrys

Beddau 'r Dewiniaid ★

A498
Campsite

Sygun
Copper Mine

8 ★

Tan-y-Mwyn

Coed
Cae-du

7

A4085

i

1

Afon Goth

2

Beddgelert

A498

Afon Glaslyn

Coed
Bryn-y-felin

3

6

Cwm Bychan

5

Pont
Aberglaslyn

Roman Fort ★

4

Nantmor

Dolfriog
Woods

A498

Nantmor Halt

A4085

Bwlchgwernog

0 ____ ¼ ____ ½ mile
0 ____ 500 m ____ 1 km

3 Cross the bridge and then take a right to cross the railway track with care. Follow the Fisherman's Path through the Aberglaslyn Pass until you reach the picturesque bridge at Aberglaslyn. Take care on this section of path as it is rough and can be slippery in sections when wet. Take special care where the path narrows around the stone buttress.

4 When you reach the bridge, bear left – don't go through the kissing gate ahead of you. Follow the path up through the ancient Celtic woodland towards the National Trust's car park at Nantmor (there are public toilets here). Continue straight ahead and go under the railway bridge.

5 Go through the picnic area and follow the path through the ancient woodland to Cwm Bychan. Along the next section of path, as you enter the cwm, you will see a wonderful waterfall with crystal clear water. From this point onwards the path will begin to climb steeply, and will be quite uneven. As you climb you will come out of the woodland onto open country.

6 The path soon becomes rocky in places, so do take care. In a while the remains of the area's copper mining industry will come into sight. There are some turnings down to the left along this section, but you need to continue straight ahead and turn to the right at the Llyn Dinas/Beddgelert waymarker.

7 The path will be quite loose underfoot with some steep sections as you drop down to Llyn Dinas. In around three-quarters of a mile (1.2 km) you will join the Llyn Dinas path. Follow this path to the left beside the Afon Glaslyn river towards Beddgelert.

8 On the way to Beddgelert, you will pass the Sygun Copper Mine attraction. Walk along the narrow road, keeping Sygun on the left, and shortly the caravan park on your right. In 500 m Beddgelert will come into sight. Go through the gate and cross the road, then follow the riverside wall back to the village centre.

The area's rich mining history can be seen in the remains of an old abandoned copper mine.

WALK 9
Cwm Idwal

Despite being only a relatively short walk from the A5 trunk road, Cwm Idwal's sense of remoteness and wilderness is awe-inspiring.

Cwm Idwal is a popular destination amongst visitors interested in walking, climbing, fishing and geology. Llyn Idwal, which lies at the bottom of the cwm, or cirque, is half a mile (800 m) long and 300 metres wide.

The cwm was formed by ice gouging the rock as glaciers thawed at the end of the last Ice Age around 12,000 years ago. It is one of the finest examples of a glacial cwm in Wales, and the folded rock of the Idwal Syncline is a world-renowned geological feature.

Legend has it that in the twelfth century, Owain, Prince of Gwynedd, decided to entrust the care of his son Idwal to his brother, Nefydd Hardd. Nefydd was envious of Idwal's intelligence and beauty, because his own son, Dunawd, did not possess the same qualities. Nefydd conspired to murder Idwal by taking him for a walk to a lake and pushing him in. Owain was devastated, and banished Nefydd from the kingdom of Gwynedd. He named the lake Llyn Idwal in memory of his son, and it is said that since that day no bird has flown over the lake, and that when there's a storm brewing in the cwm a wailing voice can be heard.

Distance: 3 miles (4.8 km)
Time: Around 2 hours
Terrain: Steep path with steps and an ascent of 460 ft (140 m)
Start/Finish: Ogwen Visitor Centre, Nant Ffrancon, Bethesda (SH 649 603)
Parking: Pay & display car park at Ogwen Warden Centre
Nearest Postcode: LL57 3LZ
Map: OS Explorer OL17 (Snowdon & Conwy Valley)

1 The route starts at the steps to the left of the Visitor Centre. Follow the path up to an iron gate which was forged by a local blacksmith, its design reflecting the landscape of Cwm Idwal.

2 Cross the wooden bridge over Afon Ogwen river and continue along the path, taking in the splendid view of mountain peaks and sharp ridges as you head towards Llyn Idwal.

3 When the path evens out, look west to enjoy the view of Nant Ffrancon valley and the slate town of Bethesda in the distance. To the east is Nant y Benglog and Llyn Ogwen.

4 Follow the prominent path on the left to walk around the lake in a clockwise direction.

5 As you walk along the path, look across the lake towards the mounds on the northern shore. These are moraines which were left behind as the glaciers thawed.

6 As you approach the southern end of the lake the path becomes gradually steeper. The slabs positioned at an angle of 50° on your left are the renowned climbing faces of Rhiwiau Caws (Idwal slabs).

7 Continue along the path and make your way up the steep steps and across the scree towards Twll Du (Devil's Kitchen). At one stage the path crosses a small waterfall. Please take care especially if it's icy as the stones can become very slippery. Once you climb the steep stone steps, you will be in the midst of the large boulders by Twll Du.

8 The path drops back down to the lake and in a while you will reach a delightful gravel beach. Continue along the path, through the gate and over the footbridge to reach the beginning of the path around the lake.

9 Retrace your steps from the lake back down to the car park.

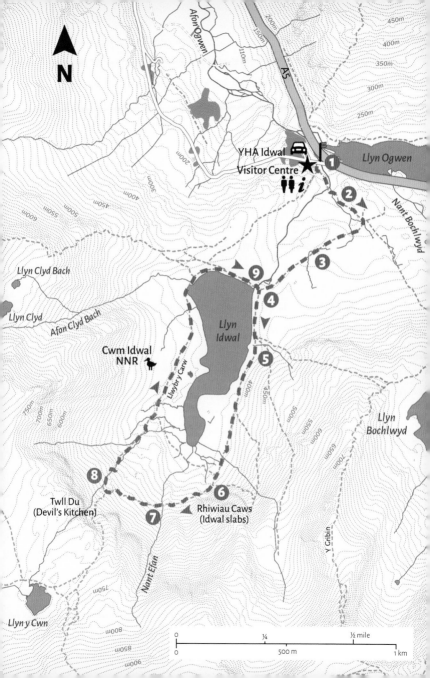

WALK 10
Dolwyddelan and Cwm Penamnen

Walk through history along a Roman road that passes medieval ruins.

Enjoy this lovely circular walk along forest tracks through the woods up to the head of the V-shaped valley of Cwm Penamnen, where you can enjoy magnificent views of the mountains of Snowdonia and the Cwm Penamnen river flowing along the valley floor. The return takes you back along part of Sarn Helen, the old Roman Road through Wales.

The last section of the walk will take you past the remains of Tai Penamnen mansion, built in the fifteenth century by Maredudd ab Ieuan ap Robert, the ancestor of the Wynns of Gwydir Castle. It is believed that Maredudd moved here from Eifionydd to escape family feuds, but now having to deal with the troublesome Ysbyty Ifan bandits instead, he moved to Gwydir Castle near Llanrwst.

Distance: 6 miles (9.6 km)
Time: Around 3 hours
Terrain: Mainly tracks and paths but with an ascent of 1,345 ft (410 m)
Start/Finish: Car park at Dolwyddelan train station (SH738 521)
Nearest Postcode: LL25 0TJ
Map: OS Explorer OL 18 (Harlech, Porthmadog & Bala)

1 At Dolwyddelan, walk along the car park approach road and turn left over the railway bridge. Once over the bridge turn left and then turn right for Cwm Penamnen passing Glan Gors street. Follow the track uphill towards the woods.

2 Continue straight ahead when you reach a junction. As you climb up the track you will go past a rock by the name of Carreg Alltrem on the left, which is very popular amongst climbers who come here to practise their skills.

3 Continue along the track until it forks, taking time to enjoy the fantastic view over Cwm Penamnen. To the right you will see the peaks of Moel Siabod, Pen yr Helgi Du, Pen Llithrig y Wrach and Carnedd y Cribau. The river, as well as the Roman road, Sarn Helen, can be seen clearly in the valley below. Take the track to the left walking up towards the head of the valley.

4 When you see yellow arrows on a sign on the left-hand side of the road, turn down the path to the right, starting your journey along the Roman road, Sarn Helen. Continue along the path down the valley, following the yellow arrows and passing a stone-built house called Tŷ'n y Cwm ('house in the valley').

5 After passing Tŷ'n y Cwm, turn right and join the tarmac road which will take you back to Dolwyddelan, passing Carreg Alltrem bridge on your right.

6 On your way back down the valley you will pass the remains of Tai Penamnen, the former mansion of Maredudd ab Ieuan ap Robert, ancestor of the Wynns of Gwydir family.

7 The road leads back to the railway bridge. Cross the bridge and turn right into the car park.

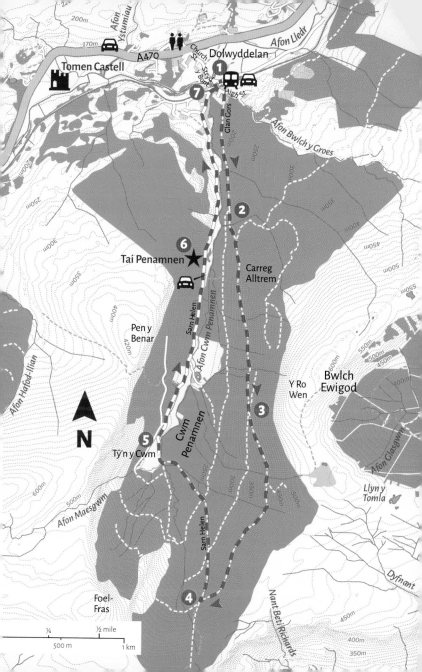

WALK 11
Cynfal Falls

Tucked away in a wooded valley, the Rhaeadr Cynfal waterfall provides a dramatic focal point to this beautiful walk.

This circular walk starts at the slate-quarrying village of Llan Ffestiniog and crosses the gently sloping countryside before descending into the spectacular gorge of the Afon Cynfal river.

The gorge was formed by glacial waters during the Ice Age, with cliffs measuring up to 130 ft (40 m) in height. The damp environment created by the rushing water provides an important habitat for ferns and other plants, and the surrounding oak woodland is now rare in Europe. The gorge forms parts of the Ceunant Cynfal National Nature Reserve and is a Site of Special Scientific Interest (SSSI), not just for its plantlife but also for its geology.

The valley is also known for its connection with the seventeenth century poet and healer Huw Llwyd, who delivered sermons from a pillar of rock in the middle of the lower falls, to congregations gathered on the river bank.

Distance: 3 miles (4.8 km)
Time: Around 2–3 hours
Start/Finish: Car park in the centre of Llan Ffestiniog (SH 701 420)
Nearest Postcode: LL41 4LR
Map: OS Explorer OL 18 (Harlech, Porthmadog & Bala)

The atmospheric falls at Cynfal
provide ideal growing conditions
for an abundance of
plant species.

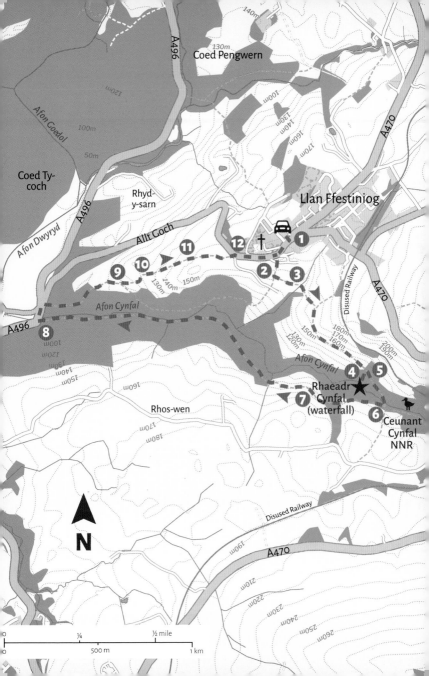

1 From the car park at Llan Ffestiniog, turn right along the main road (B4391) and continue down the road towards the church. Cross the road with care and continue downhill until you see a gate signed "Rhaeadr Cynfal Falls". Follow the path down a few steps and through a small gate.

2 Continue through the field (sheep and cattle may be encountered, so dogs need to be kept on leads) and follow the public footpath sign to the left through a metal gate. Walk between the tree and the outbuilding and across the field towards a yellow pole, which leads you down towards a small metal gate and footbridge.

3 Continue along the path to another metal gate and follow the stone wall, keeping it on your left. Go through a wooden gate and turn right. Go through another wooden gate on the left and then follow the fence on your left-hand side. Continue along the path, heading downhill through a wooden gate and towards the woods.

4 Enter the woodland through the wooden gate – the viewpoint for the Cynfal waterfall can be reached by following the path down to the right.

5 To continue along the walk, retrace your steps back to the main path and turn right. The path leads to a bridge over Afon Cynfal.

6 Cross the bridge and turn right through a gate at the top of the steps and follow the path through two small wooden gates (this section of the path can be very wet in places).

7 Follow the waymarkers which will direct you through a number of gates. Continue along the path and you will eventually reach the main road.

8 Turn right and continue over the bridge, being mindful of the traffic, until you see a public footpath sign and a stile on the right. Climb over the stile and follow the path up through the woods.

9 At the fork in the path, bear left and continue up to a stile. Climb over and follow a stone wall into the open countryside. Go through a gap in the wall and follow the path that leads uphill towards an electricity pylon.

10 When the path forks, bear right through a wooden gate and follow the path, keeping the fence to your left and the pylon to your right.

11 Carry on straight ahead, through the gate, and continue towards the main road, heading towards another gate.

12 On reaching the main road, turn right and retrace your steps back to the car park.

WALK 12

Farchynys

A wonderful short walk through a native woodland on the southern edge of the Mawddach estuary.

Farchynys woodland is situated in a beautiful spot on the southern edge of the Mawddach estuary, with far-reaching views across vast and beautiful marshland. Various vantage points throughout the woodland offer magnificent views of the Barmouth wooden railway bridge, the estuary and the peaks of Cader Idris and other mountains beyond.

The woodland boasts a mixture of native trees including oak, birch, ash, rowan, sycamore and holly, and from late spring to early summer the woodland floor is carpeted with bluebells. Farchynys is also home to a diversity of woodland birds such as the pied flycatcher, tree creeper and nuthatch. In spring, the call of the cuckoo can also be heard.

Along the route through the woodland you will see a small mine adit – this is one of many test adits in the area that were created in the search for gold veins. The Dolgellau area has a long history of gold mining dating back to the nineteenth century, with the largest and most renowned mine being the Clogau mine. After the initial goldrush between 1860 and 1911, smaller-scale gold mining recommenced at the mine for a brief nine-year period between 1989 and 1998. To this day, jewellery containing gold from this mine continues to be sold worldwide.

Distance: 1 mile (1.6 km)
Time: Around 1 hour
Terrain: Woodland paths and minor roads/tracks.
Start/Finish: Farchynys car park, near Bont-ddu (SH 662 186)
Nearest Postcode: LL42 1TN
Map: OS Explorer OL23 (Cader Idris & Llyn Tegid)

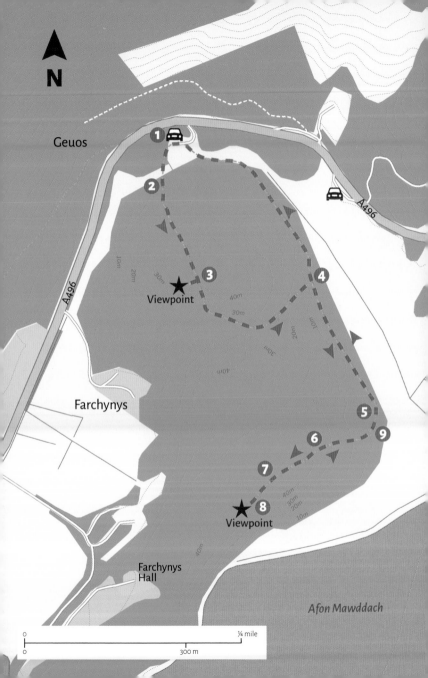

1 Standing in the Farchynys car park facing the woodland, walk over the grassy area towards the entrance to the woodland on the right-hand side.

2 Follow the path between the trees, and when you reach a fork in the path, bear right to access the viewpoint. From here you will be able to see Barmouth wooden railway bridge and lovely views of the Mawddach estuary between the oak trees.

3 Retrace your steps from the viewpoint back to the fork in the path. Turn right here.

4 When you reach a wide track, turn right. At high tide the marshland on your left often floods. Keep an eye on the reeds as you walk along – you may catch sight of some of the area's resident wildlife!

5 At the end of the track you will come to an open area with a picnic table and far-reaching views of the estuary towards Dolgellau and across towards Cader Idris beyond. On the right in front of you there is a gate and stile, do not go over the stile. Turn right and follow the path along the fence line up through the woods.

6 When you reach a fork in the path, bear left.

7 When you reach a fence, turn left to access the viewpoint and admire the spectacular view of Cader Idris and the estuary below.

8 Retrace your steps from the viewpoint back to the fence, turn right and follow the path back down through the woods to the picnic area at the end of the track.

9 Follow the track to the left, and continue straight ahead, going through two kissing gates, until you arrive back at the car park.

Looking towards Cader Idris from the top of Farchynys Woods.

WALK 13
Foel Caerynwch

*The summit of Foel Caerynwch offers
awe-inspiring panoramic views of the
hills of Meirionnydd.*

Foel Caerynwch summit is a fine place to see how this
landscape was formed by glaciers scouring their way
westwards to join the huge ice sheet that lay between Wales
and Ireland. This hill would have been in a fork between
two glaciers, avoiding the worst of the erosion. The large
boulders in the Clywedog river below and on the path there
are testament to the great forces which plucked them from
the mountains above, depositing them there when the ice
eventually melted about 10,000 years ago.

This path is a great place for seeing hovering kestrels and
soaring buzzards, so it's worth bringing a pair of binoculars
along with you. In early summer you may hear the distinctive
call of the cuckoo.

Distance: 2 miles (3.2 km)
Time: Around 1½ hours
Ascent: 570 ft (175 m)
Terrain: Fields and some rough, wet terrain.
Start/Finish: Brithdir village hall (SH 771 188)
Parking: Lay-by opposite Brithdir village hall
Nearest Postcode: LL40 2RR
Map: OS Explorer OL23 (Cader Idris & Llyn Tegid)

1 From Brithdir village hall, walk along the pavement towards the bus stop. Enjoy the view of Foel Caerynwch on your left.

2 Turn left before the chapel onto a road with a 'No through road' sign. Pass Cefn y Maes on your left and go through the gate in front of you and head towards Ty'n Llidiart. You will see an impressive view of Cader Idris on your right.

3 After passing Ty'n Llidiart, follow the grassy track up to the left. Go through the gate and follow the waymarkers uphill.

4 Turn left following the signpost for Foel Caerynwch and keep to the Permissive Path. When you reach a gate, follow the path signposted Foel Caerynwch which runs alongside the stone wall.

5 Turn right, following the waymarker and still following the line of the stone wall. Then follow the waymarker to the left and walk along the path which crosses the field and then zigzags uphill towards a stile.

6 Climb over the stile on to open access land, turn left and follow the white posts uphill. When you reach the third post you are almost at the summit of Foel Caerynwch. Walk straight uphill to the summit where you can enjoy spectacular views of Meirionnydd and beyond.

7 To make your way down from the summit, follow the white posts to the east across the open access land for a quarter of a mile (400 m) until you reach a stile.

8 Go over the stile and turn right, following the posts towards a gap in the wall. (This area can be very wet at times.) Follow the white posts that lead you along a faint path which zigzags downhill around the hawthorn trees.

9 At the bottom of the field, go over the stile next to the gate, keep right and walk along the edge of the field, heading towards a pole in the far corner.

10 Follow the public footpath sign on the gatepost in front of you (ignoring the public footpath sign pointing to the right). Keep following this path as it approaches the village and joins a gravel track.

11 Go over the stile next to the gate, turn left and walk along the road back to the start of the walk, passing the earthworks of Brithdir Roman fort to your right.

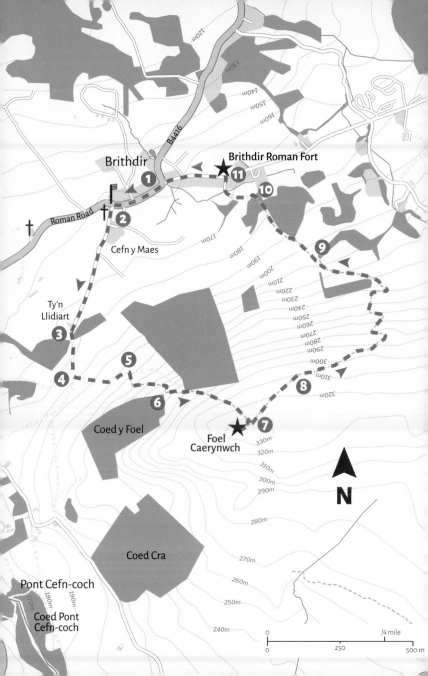

A short but fairly strenuous walk leads to the summit of Foel Caerynwch.

WALK 14
Foel Offrwm

Enjoy 360° views of an area steeped in folklore as you skirt around Foel Offrwm or 'The Hill of Sacrifice'.

This is a new path on the Nannau estate near Llanfachreth on the outskirts of Dolgellau. Thanks to the cooperation of the landowner, this easy circular walk, which offers spectacular views of south Meirionnydd, has recently been reopened. The initial section up to the first viewpoint is suitable for wheelchairs.

The walk roughly follows the 800 ft (250 m) contour around the foot of Foel Offrwm hill. The views are ever-changing as you circle the hill, and include the Georgian mansion of Plas Nannau, the mountain ranges of Cader Idris, Aran and Rhinogydd, the Mawddach estuary and even as far as Mount Snowdon on a clear day.

This walk can be combined with Walk 18 (Precipice Walk) to form a longer, figure-of-eight route.

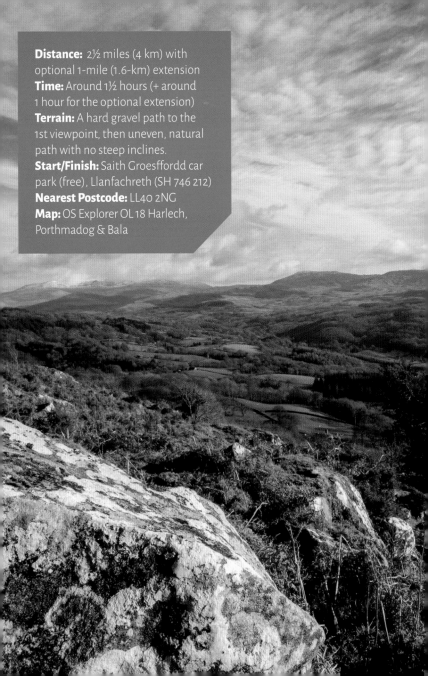

Distance: 2½ miles (4 km) with optional 1-mile (1.6-km) extension
Time: Around 1½ hours (+ around 1 hour for the optional extension)
Terrain: A hard gravel path to the 1st viewpoint, then uneven, natural path with no steep inclines.
Start/Finish: Saith Groesffordd car park (free), Llanfachreth (SH 746 212)
Nearest Postcode: LL40 2NG
Map: OS Explorer OL 18 Harlech, Porthmadog & Bala

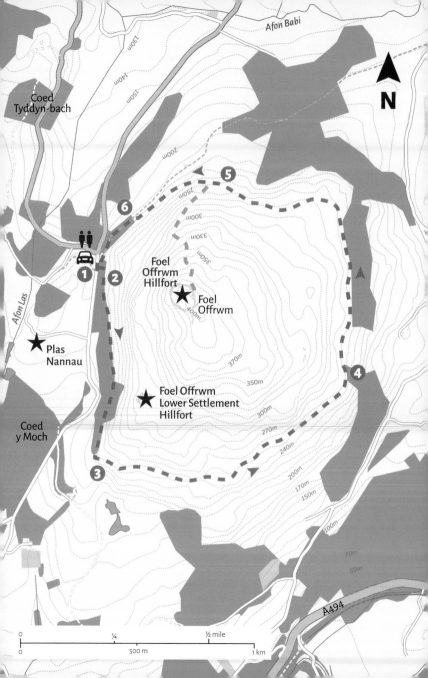

Afon Babi

N

Coed
Tyddyn-bach

130m

140m

150m

200m

250m

300m

330m

5

6

350m

400m

Foel
Offrwm
Hillfort

★ Foel
Offrwm

1

2

Afon Las

★ Plas
Nannau

370m

350m

300m

270m

★ Foel Offrwm
Lower Settlement
Hillfort

240m

Coed
y Moch

200m

170m

150m

100m

70m

50m

3

4

A494

0   ¼   ½ mile

0   500 m   1 km

1 Carefully cross the road from the upper end of the Saith Groesffordd car park and turn right onto a gravel path that rises through the trees towards a wooden gate. The path continues to rise for a short distance but then it is quite even. This section is suitable for wheelchairs.

2 Follow the path through the striking beech and oak woodland, and notice Plas Nannau to your right. After around half a mile (800 m) you will reach a bench which is an ideal spot to sit down and admire the view of Cader Idris rising majestically above the town of Dolgellau. Below you is the estate's former deer park. The accessible section of path ends here.

3 Continue straight ahead and climb the oak steps by the small quarry, and make your way through two further gates until you reach the southern face of Foel Offrwm and its rowan trees and hawthorn. You may see the yellowhammer on this section.

4 When you reach the conifer plantation, follow the fence to the left. You will cross wetter ground over a rough stone path. After passing the trees, the former volcano of Rhobell Fawr will come into sight, and the village of Llanfachreth in the hollow below. If you are quiet enough you may catch a glimpse of a deer on this section.

5 You will now be heading back towards the car park.

Optional extension: If you wish to climb to the summit of Foel Offrwm, there is a path on your left, with a boulder marking the starting point. There is a bench about half way to the summit, where you can enjoy the view of the Garn and Rhinogydd and out towards the sea. You will need to retrace your steps back down here to continue on the circular walk.

6 The circular walk ends by going through a wooden gate and joining one of the old roads that led to Plas Nannau mansion, which takes you back to the car park.

WALK 15
Y Garn

Y Garn is a fine little summit. It punches way above its weight view-wise and puts many loftier peaks to shame.

This route will take you through an ancient oak woodland – renowned for its mosses, lichens, ferns and liverworts and abundant wildlife – before emerging onto the open mountain.

The Cefn Coch gold mine on the slopes of Y Garn was operational between 1864 and 1914 and was the third richest in the district after Clogau and Gwynfynydd. You will see the fenced-off workings on the grassy ridge of Cefn Coch as you approach the upper mine.

The final part of the route to the summit is much rougher, being heathery, wet and rocky, and can be difficult to navigate in poor weather. Map-reading skills are therefore essential for this walk.

The summit views are stupendous: the northern Snowdonia giants, then panning eastwards to Arenig Fawr, Aran Benllyn, Aran Fawddwy, Cader Idris, the Mawddach estuary. To the west, the view is dominated by the long ridge line of the Rhinogydd.

1 Starting at the National Trust car park in Ganllwyd village, cross the main road (A470) with care and walk through the Coed Ganllwyd Nature Reserve to the footbridge.

2 Walk past the impressive mine buildings and along to the mine itself.

3 Admire the wonderful views back down towards the village and Coed y Brenin forest.

4 Follow the broad, grassy ridge, passing many fenced-off workings, to the uppermost mine of Cefn Coch.

5 Continue, climbing steeply up the hillside above the mine to the wall junction.

6 The going gets rougher now. Follow the wall northwest to the stile. Cross the stile and follow the wall southwest to the junction.

7 Climb gently in a northwesterly direction for 1,300 ft (400 m) to the summit, where you will be rewarded with spectacular views.

8 Return to your starting point by retracing your steps.

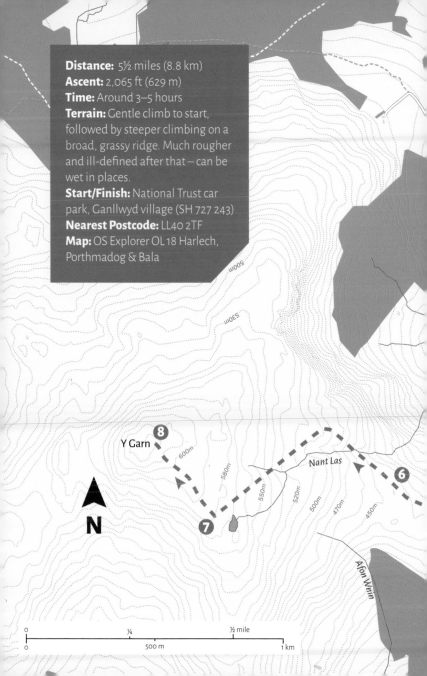

Distance: 5½ miles (8.8 km)
Ascent: 2,065 ft (629 m)
Time: Around 3–5 hours
Terrain: Gentle climb to start, followed by steeper climbing on a broad, grassy ridge. Much rougher and ill-defined after that – can be wet in places.
Start/Finish: National Trust car park, Ganllwyd village (SH 727 243)
Nearest Postcode: LL40 2TF
Map: OS Explorer OL18 Harlech, Porthmadog & Bala

Y Garn ⑧

600m

Nant Las

⑥

580m

550m

520m

500m

470m

450m

⑦

530m

530m

500m

Afon Wnin

N

0   ¼   ½ mile
0   500 m   1 km

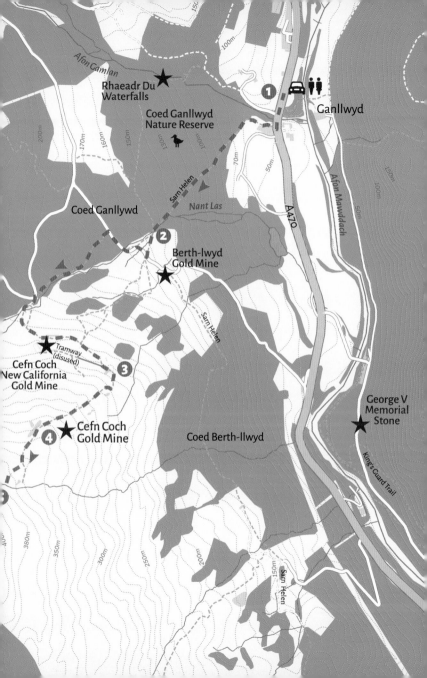

Rhaeadr Du
Waterfalls

Coed Ganllwyd
Nature Reserve

Ganllwyd

Coed Ganllwyd

Sarn Helen

Nant Las

2

Berth-lwyd
Gold Mine

Tramway
(disused)

Cefn Coch
New California
Gold Mine

3

Sarn Helen

George V
Memorial
Stone

Cefn Coch
Gold Mine

4

Coed Berth-llwyd

King's Guard Trail

Sarn Helen

1

A470

Afon Camlan

Afon Mawddach

200m
170m
160m
150m
150m
130m
100m
70m
50m

150m
100m
50m

380m
350m
300m
250m
200m
200m
150m

Sunset behind Rhinogydd from Y Garn summit. Y Garn is one of the Welsh 3000s: fifteen peaks that reach heights of over 3,000 ft (914 m).

WALK 16

Llyn Gwynant

A wonderful walk in the foothills of Snowdon, affording spectacular views of Llyn Gwynant and the surrounding mountains.

If you want to walk in the Snowdon area during peak season but prefer to avoid the crowds, then this lovely circular walk is a good option. Beginning at Nant Gwynant on the southern foothill of Snowdon, the walk will take you up to the hills adjacent, offering spectacular views of Moel Hebog, yr Aran, Snowdon and Llyn Gwynant, and the Glyderau.

The walk around the lake itself may seem familiar to Tomb Raider fans, as the Lara Croft sequel, *The Temple of Doom* was filmed on the shores of Llyn Gwynant in 2003. This was not the first time that the area was used as a filming location for blockbuster films – the slopes of Snowdon to the west of Llyn Gwynant doubled as the Khyber Pass in the 1968 film *Carry On Up the Khyber.*

Distance: Around 5½ miles (8.8 km)
Time: Around 3–4 hours
Terrain: Paths and tracks, can be wet
Start/Finish: SNPA car park (pay & display), Nant Gwynant (SH 627 506)
Nearest Postcode: LL55 4NR
Map: OS Explorer OL17 (Snowdon & Conwy Valley)

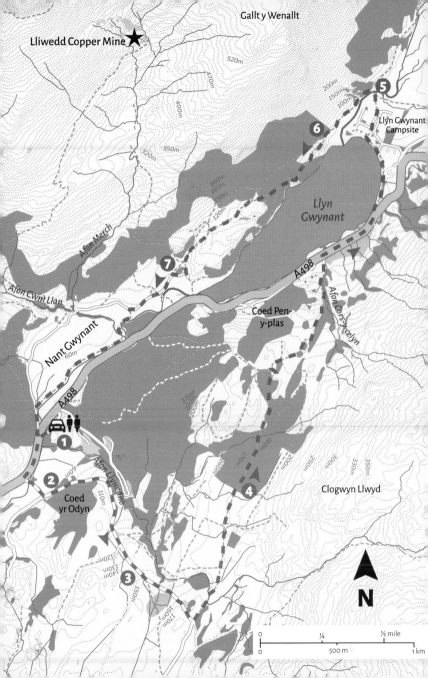

Lliwedd Copper Mine ★

Gallt y Wenallt

520m

400m

120m

200m
150m
100m

⑤

Llyn Gwynant
Campsite

⑥

350m

320m

Afon Merch

200m
180m
150m

120m

Llyn
Gwynant

Afon Cwm Llan

⑦

A498

Coed Pen-
y-plas

Afon Cors-y-celyn

Nant Gwynant
60m

A498

230m
200m

190m

A498

①

Afon Llynedno

②

Coed
yr Odyn

110m

120m
130m

④

Clogwyn Llwyd

150m

170m
160m

③

160m

200m

250m

300m

170m

160m

200m

250m

300m

330m

350m

N

0   ¼   ½ mile

0   500 m   1 km

1 From the car park at Nant Gwynant cross the road and walk along the pavement towards Beddgelert. After a third of a mile (500 m), turn left into the back road to Nantmor. Pass the entrance to Llyndy Farm, and then continue past Castell Farm, after which there is a sharp right-hand bend. Follow the public footpath to the left from here.

2 The path leads to Afon Llynedno river. Cross the timber bridge and follow the path across the field. From here you will enjoy a wonderful view towards Moel Hebog, Yr Aran, Snowdon and Y Glyderau.

3 You will reach a small gate and a timber boardwalk. The path runs through Coed yr Eryr woods before joining an old farm track on the other side. It will take you past an old agricultural barn before affording you a view of Llyn Gwynant.

4 Follow the track down to the main road, turn right and follow the road for about a third of a mile (500 m). Follow the path that leads around the lake shore towards Llyn Gwynant Campsite. Public footpath signs will guide you through the campsite to a stone bridge over Afon Glaslyn river.

5 Cross the bridge and follow the path to the left through the woods before climbing up Penamnen precipice, which is an ideal spot to take a break and enjoy the magnificent view across Llyn Gwynant.

6 Continue through the woods before climbing over a stile which takes you on to quite wet terrain. Once past this section you will reach a point where you will be looking down Nant Gwynant with Coed yr Eryr on the left and Afon Glaslyn leading you back to the car park.

7 Follow the path until you reach the Hafod y Llan farm track. After passing some old ruins, cross the field to a timber bridge. From here you will see the path leading along the river towards the car park.

WALK 17
Panorama Walk

A wonderfully varied walk in the uplands above the seaside town of Barmouth, offering amazing views of the Mawddach estuary.

This varied circular walk provides some of the most spectacular views in Snowdonia. Visitors have been enjoying parts of this walk since the Victorian period, taking in the splendid views of the Mawddach estuary, the Cader Idris mountain range and out towards Cardigan Bay.

The first part of the walk up to the Panorama Walk viewpoint, is easy and suitable for young families, but there are steep sections beyond this point. The path can also be quite wet in places, so waterproof footwear is recommended.

The route will take you past old Victorian gardens, once a very popular attraction amongst the visitors to Barmouth, and an old derelict building that used to be a tea room for visitors.

Towards the end of the walk you will pass the crags of Garn, often referred to as the 'Barmouth Slabs', which is a popular spot for rock climbing.

Distance: 4 miles (6.4 km)
Time: Around 3–4 hours
Terrain: Fields, woods and some rough and wet terrain.
Start/Finish: SNPA car park 1 mile (1.6 km) from Barmouth (SH 625 166)
Nearest Postcode: LL42 1DJ
Map: OS Explorer OL23 (Cader Idris & Llyn Tegid)

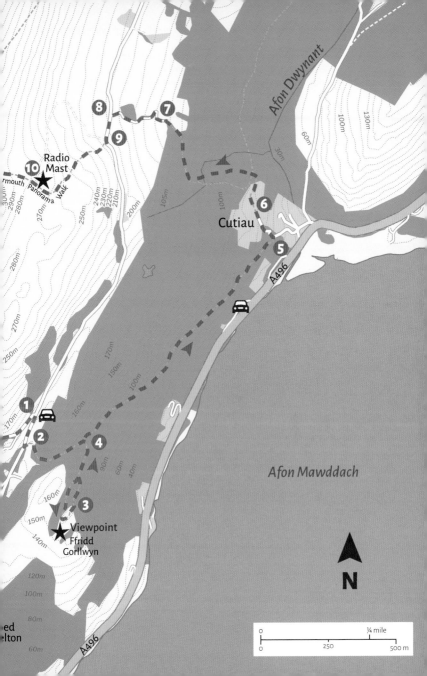

Afon Dwynant

130m

100m

60m

30m

105m

100m

⑧

⑨

⑦

Radio
Mast

⑩
rmouth   Panorama   Walk

300m
290m
280m
270m

250m

240m
230m
220m
210m

200m

280m

270m

250m

170m

150m

100m

⑥

Cutiau

⑤

A496

160m

170m

170m

①

②

④

90m
60m
40m

160m

③

150m

140m

Viewpoint
Ffridd
Gorllwyn

120m

100m

80m

60m

ed
·lton

A496

Afon Mawddach

N

0		¼ mile
0	250	500 m

1 From the car park, walk downhill towards Barmouth and shortly turn left following the 'Panorama Walk' signpost. Go through a gate and follow the grassy track.

2 The old road takes you to woodland. Go through the gate ahead of you and then through another gate on your right, still following signs for 'Panorama Walk'. This path will take you on a short detour to the Panorama Walk viewpoint. Keep to the left while ascending through the trees to the rocky summit.

3 Once you've had time to enjoy the splendid views, walk onwards around the rocky summit and down the narrow path on the other side. Walk back to the gate near the old road.

4 To continue the walk, turn right and rejoin the old road, (the path can be very wet here). Follow the old road for just over half a mile (1 km) as it descends to the village of Cutiau, passing the old Victorian gardens on your right.

5 When you reach a tarmac road, turn left and walk up the hill to the small village of Cutiau. The road in front of you splits three ways. Follow the track in the middle that has a public footpath sign on the fence. As you reach an old chapel follow the path on your right and go through the gate.

6 Once past the chapel, follow the public footpath until you reach a junction beneath the electricity cables. Follow the narrow path to the left which climbs steeply through the woods and uphill. (The path can be very wet here.) Go through two gates.

7 The path joins a tarmac road as it goes past a dwelling with old farm buildings. Follow the road until you reach a junction.

8 At the T-junction turn left and walk along the road for about 100 meters.

9 As you pass a turning on your right, follow the public footpath sign uphill between the two stone walls on your right. Cross the stile and follow the path towards the radio mast, heading through a gate.

10 Keep right at the fork in the path near the radio mast, walking around it and along the line of the stone wall. Go through the gate next to the stile (leaving it as you found it – either open or closed) and follow the faint path which climbs steeply uphill to the pass of Bwlch y Llan.

11 As you reach Bwlch y Llan, go through the gate and continue along the narrow path ahead. Shortly, turn left to join the Taith Ardudwy Way path.

12 Follow the path to the far end of the pass. (The path can be very wet here.) Follow the path to the left which heads towards a gate. Go through the gate and follow the wide path for a while until you reach a small farm, Gellfawr.

13 At Gellfawr, walk past the front of the house and follow the grassy road. Go over the stile and follow the road that will shortly take you past the crags of Garn on your right.

14 Go over the last stile of this walk and follow the road down to the car park.

WALK 18
Precipice Walk

A truly breathtaking walk that skirts around the slope of Moel Cynwch at a height of 800 ft (250 m), offering spectacular views of the surrounding countryside.

Thanks to the kind permission of the Nannau Estate, the public have been granted permission to enjoy this walk over the estate's land since 1890, on the understanding that they observe the countryside code, keep dogs on a lead, follow the route indicated and use the proper access.

The Precipice Walk is one of Dolgellau's most renowned attractions. The route takes you through an interesting variety of habitats including a deciduous woodland, a conifer plantation, meadows, along a lakeside and on sheep tracks. But the walk's main attraction is the incomparable view down the Mawddach estuary and of the principal mountain ranges of Snowdonia. To the north are Yr Wyddfa (Snowdon) and the Moelwynion, to the west is the Rhinogydd, immediately south is the long scarp of Cader Idris, while the Aran and Arenig can be seen to the east.

It is a contour walk in that the path roughly follows the level of the 800-ft (250-m) contour line, so there is not much climbing or descending involved, making it ideal for the whole family. The precipice, along part of the western side, is not as terrifying as it sounds, although walkers who suffer from vertigo may need some assistance along this section.

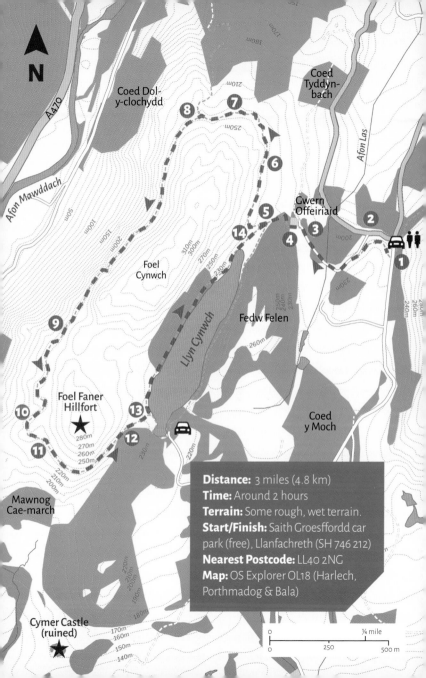

N

Coed Dol-
y-clochydd

Coed Tyddyn-
bach

⑧

⑦

Afon Mawddach

A470

⑥

Gwern
Offeiriaid

②

⑤

③

⑭

④

①

Foel
Cynwch

Fedw Felen

Llyn Cynwch

⑨

Foel Faner
Hillfort
★

Coed
y Moch

⑩

⑬

⑪

⑫

Mawnog
Cae-march

Cymer Castle
(ruined)
★

Distance: 3 miles (4.8 km)
Time: Around 2 hours
Terrain: Some rough, wet terrain.
Start/Finish: Saith Groesffordd car park (free), Llanfachreth (SH 746 212)
Nearest Postcode: LL40 2NG
Map: OS Explorer OL18 (Harlech, Porthmadog & Bala)

0   ¼ mile
0   250   500 m

1 Leave the Saith Groesffordd car park at the upper end, where there is a path to the right through Coed Cefndiwiog.

2 After around 250 m follow the lane to the left.

3 Continue for a further 300 m, following the path left, past Gwern Offeiriaid house.

4 Follow the path up and to the right through the woods. After 100 m go through a gate into an open field.

5 Follow the path towards Llyn Cynwch lake. Before you reach the lake, turn right up the hill following the stone wall.

6 Continue to follow the path along the stone wall. In the parkland on the right, there are a number of ancient oak trees that sustain important populations of lichens and mosses.

7 After nearly a quarter of a mile (350 m), go through a gap in a stone wall where you will soon have fine views looking north over Coed y Brenin forest.

8 Follow the path to the left at the signpost, heading towards the old copper mine of Glasdir.

9 Follow the path for just over half a mile (1 km), taking in the views of the Afon Mawddach river in the valley below, until you reach a wooden gate.

10 Go through the gate and continue along the path for another 500 m until you reach the mouth of the valley with spectacular views of the Mawddach estuary.

11 Continue along the path through a gate in the stone wall.

12 After nearly a third of a mile (500 m), go through another gate in a stone wall and continue down towards Llyn Cynwch.

13 When you reach Llyn Cynwch, turn left and follow the path around the northern edge of the lake.

14 At the end of the lake, rejoin the path you started on. Retrace your steps back to the car park.

The Precipice Walk offers stunning views over the Mawddach valley.

WALK 19
Tomen y Mur

A lovely walk to one of the country's most complete examples of a Roman military settlement.

This circular walk will take you from the shores of the Llyn Trawsfynydd reservoir, across farmland to the remains of the Roman fort of Tomen y Mur.

Tomen y Mur is one of the most interesting archeological sites in Snowdonia, and is one of the most complete Roman military settlements in Britain. The fort is situated on a hillside at the crossroads of four Roman roads and offers commanding views of the local area. It was constructed in AD 78 by Gnaeus Julius Agricola, a Roman general responsible for much of the Roman conquest of Britain, to maintain order amongst the natives and protect road communications.

The walk starts from the entrance to the Trawsfynydd Nuclear Power Station. Construction of the power station began in 1959 and the plant generated electricity for twenty-six years between 1965 and 1991. Today, the lengthy decommissioning process is underway, and likely to continue for many years to come.

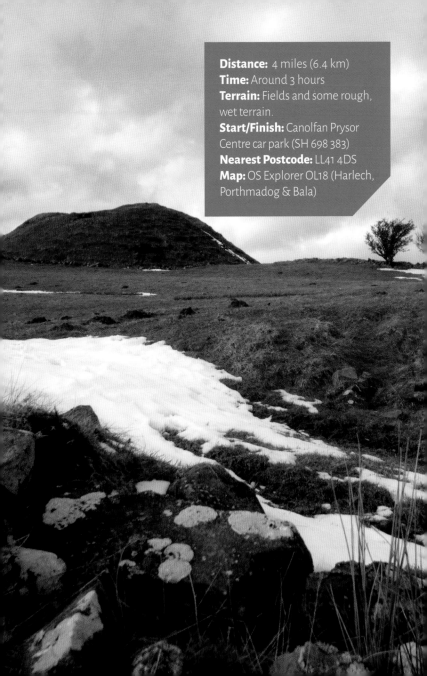

Distance: 4 miles (6.4 km)
Time: Around 3 hours
Terrain: Fields and some rough, wet terrain.
Start/Finish: Canolfan Prysor Centre car park (SH 698 383)
Nearest Postcode: LL41 4DS
Map: OS Explorer OL18 (Harlech, Porthmadog & Bala)

1 Aim for the far end of Canolfan Prysor Centre car park where you can pick up the cycle path. Follow the cycle path for just over a mile (1.6 km) until you reach the A470 highway.

2 Cross the A470 highway, taking due care as this is a very busy road. Follow the country road opposite for about 50 m and cross the bridge on your left. Follow the path through two gates. At the tarmac road, turn right and continue for 300 m until you reach an old railway bridge.

3 Cross the bridge, and turn left by the Public Footpath sign. Follow the track uphill and in 200 m go through a gate. Keep following the track and go through another gate. As you reach a bend follow the track uphill towards the pylon in front of you.

4 At the next gate turn right, keeping the fence on your left. Walk uphill, aiming between the pylon and the ruins of an old building. Follow the path and go through a gate. Cross the bridge over the stream and walk through a gap in the wall.

5 Before you reach the next gate, look out for a small gate in the stone wall on your left signed 'Tomen y Mur'. Go through the gate and cross the open land towards the old fort from where you can enjoy wonderful panoramic views.

6 From the fort's mound, aim towards the reconstructed section of the fort's wall, and walk through the ruins of an old farmhouse. Look at that amazing fireplace!

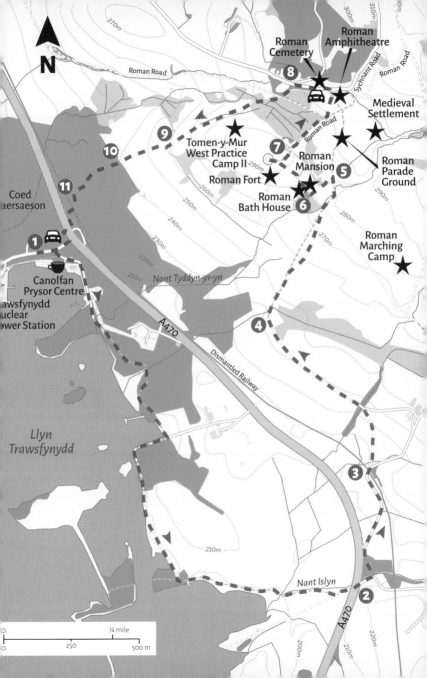

N

Roman Cemetery
Roman Amphitheatre

Roman Road

⑧

Medieval Settlement

Sychnant Road

Roman Road

Roman Road

⑨

Tomen-y-Mur West Practice Camp II

⑦

Roman Mansion

Roman Parade Ground

⑩

Roman Fort

Roman Bath House

⑥

⑤

⑪

Coed aersaeson

①

Roman Marching Camp

Canolfan Prysor Centre

awsfynydd uclear ower Station

A470

Nant Tyddyn-yr-yn

④

Dismantled Railway

Llyn Trawsfynydd

③

210m

Nant Islyn

②

A470

¼ mile

250   500 m

Ruins of a fort and farmhouse make up part of Tomen y Mur Roman archeological site.

7 Follow the grassy track across the field towards the Tomen y Mur car park. From the car park follow the tarmac road down to the left.

8 In about 100 m cross the stile next to the Public Footpath sign on your left. Walk down through the trees to a stone bridge and cross another stile. Walk towards the electricity pylon, aiming for two gates at the far end of the field.

9 Go through the gate and follow the path downhill. Go through another gate near the pylon, and walk downhill keeping the fence on your left.

10 Go through the gate and follow the indistinct path down through the woodland towards the electricity pylon. Keep left (don't go over the strange wooden stile over a wall). When you reach a wall at the bottom of the woodland, follow the path to the left towards a gate.

11 Go through the gate and through the tunnel under the old railway line. Climb the steps up to a lay-by on the A470. Cross the road, exercising due care, and walk to the left along the pavement. Turn right towards the Trawsfynydd Decomissioning Site and walk back to the car park.

WALK 20
Torrent Walk, Dolgellau

A wonderful walk, best enjoyed in spring or early summer when the woodland floor is carpeted with bluebells and the smell of wild garlic fills the air.

This circular walk through the striking gorge of Afon Clywedog river is one of the most popular routes in the Dolgellau area. Originally, the path was built by Thomas Payne and his son; he was also the designer of the Cob across Afon Glaslyn river in Porthmadog. The work was commissioned by Baron Richards of the mansion Plas Caerynwch, which is further up the river, in order to extend the mansion's gardens.

More recently, the Snowdonia National Park Authority has restored the old path on the eastern side of the gorge, keeping to the route of the original path where possible. As the whole gorge has been designated a Site of Special Scientific Interest (SSSI), care had to be taken during the restoration work to ensure that the fragile environment was not damaged.

At one time the banks of the river Clywedog were bursting with industrial activity. There was a fulling mill, a smithy, a woollen mill and an iron furnace – some of which are still here today. The gorge also has a wealth of wildlife and special plants – there are otters, dormice and lesser horseshoe bats not to mention an important collection of mosses, lichen, ferns, fungi and liverwort.

Distance: 2½ miles (4 km)
Time: Around 1–2 hours
Terrain: Rough, steep sections.
Start/Finish: Lay-by near the village of Brithdir on the B4416 (SH 761 182)
Nearest Postcode: LL40 2RH
Map: OS Explorer OL23 (Cader Idris & Llyn Tegid)

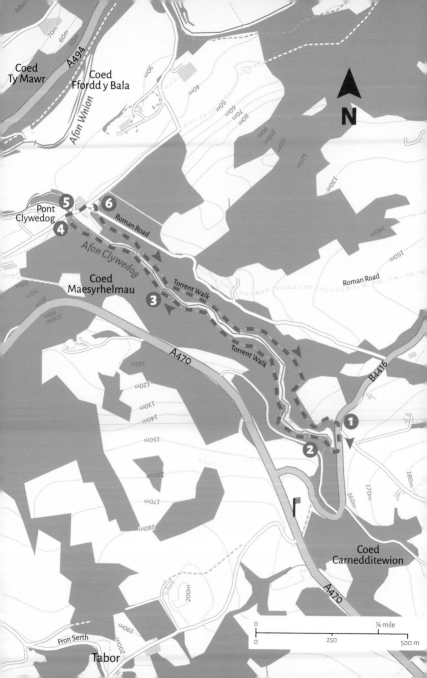

1 From the lay-by, walk back along the main road towards Pont ar Ddibyn for 100 m passing the first signpost for Torrent Walk and taking care of the traffic. Near the second oak signpost for Torrent Walk, turn right through the kissing gate. You will be crossing a wooden bridge over the gorge.

2 Soon you can take a seat on a bench commemorated to Mary Richards, the well-known botanist who used to live at Plas Caerynwch further upstream.

3 Further down the gorge you will see three large boulders across the path. These were deposited here by glaciers around 10,000 years ago. Notice the abundance of ivy, fern and mosses covering the broadleaved trees above – oak, beech and ash trees. Important collections of lichens and liverworts also grow here.

4 Soon you will reach the bottom road. A short distance from Pont Clywedog bridge towards Dolgellau are the ruins of an old iron furnace dating back to the early eighteenth century. It was built by Abraham Darby, the Quaker from Coalbrookdale. He and other Quakers from Dolserau and Dolgun farms used to mine iron ore on nearby Tir Stent and haul it down to the furnace. If you do have time, take a detour to explore the ruins. You will need to walk about 150 m along the country road towards Dolgellau from Pont Clywedog.

5 To continue along Torrent Walk, turn right over Pont Clywedog. The buildings on your right were previously a woollen mill and warehouse. Water to power the mill was taken from the river further upstream; some of the structure can be seen today.

6 Keep to your right at the fork in front of you and walk up the hill until you reach another signpost. Follow the path along the gorge up to the car park.

Picturesque stone bridge over the river Clywedog on the Torrent Walk.

Acknowledgements

Thanks to all of the photographers who allowed us to use their imagery in this book.

page 6 © Gwen Edwards; 9 © Linda George/shutterstock; 12 © Gail Johnson/shutterstock; 22-23 © SNPA; 26-27 ©APCE/SNPA; 31 ©APCE/SNPA; 35 © SNPA; 38-39 © Myfyr Tomos; 44-45 © Julia Gavin/ Alamy Stock Photo; 50-51 © Pearl Bucknall/Alamy Stock Photo; 56-57 © Gwen Aeron Edwards; 59 © SNPA; 62-63 © Coollife/Alamy Stock Photo; 65 © Gwen Aeron Edwards; 69 © Gwen Aeron Edwards;73 © CW Images/Alamy Stock Photo; 74 © Dave Ellison/Alamy Stock Photo; 79 ©APCE/SNPA; 82-83 © Gwen Edwards; 85 © H Lansdown/Alamy Stock Photo; 89 ©APCE/SNPA; 91 © Gwen Aeron Edwards; 98-99 © Myfyr Tomos; 101 © Gwen Aeron Edwards; 105 © APCE/SNPA; 114-115 © SNPA; 117 © Alwyn Jonrs/Alamy Stock Photo; 120 © David Angel/ Alamy Stock Photo; 123 © Andrew Kearton/Alamy Stock Photo; 126-127 © David Hall Photography/Alamy Stock Photo

SNPA (Snowdonia National Park Authority)

Maps © OpenStreetMap contributors
Contains OS data © Crown copyright [and database right] 2020.
Map creation: Cosmographics Ltd (www.cosmographics.co.uk).
Page design and layout: mapuccino (mapuccino.com.au).
Edited by Karen Marland.